Dear Peter,

over many

MY ARCHITECTURE

Oscar Niemeyer

Editora Revan

English version:
Ricardo Antonio
Denilson Freitas

Revising:
Dalva Silveira
Wendell Setúbal

Printing:
Ebal
(On Top Print 90g paper, after electronic paging in Garamond font, sizes 13/16)

CIP-Brasil. Catalogued

Sindicato Nacional dos Editores de Livros, RJ
(National Syndicate of Book Publishers, Rio de Janeiro)

N575m Niemeyer, Oscar, 1907 –
My Architecture / Oscar Niemeyer – Rio de Janeiro
Revan, 2000
112 pages

ISBN 85-706-199-8

1 – Niemeyer, Oscar, 1907 - . 2 . Arquitetura Moderna –
Século XX – Brasil. 1. Título.

00-1030.   CDD   720.981
                                              CDU   72(81)

280700   310700   009353

*The most important thing for me is not architecture, but family,
friends and this unfair world that we need to change.*

I will make the beginning saying that my name should have been Oscar Ribeiro Almeida de Niemeyer Soares. Ribeiro and Soares, Portuguese names. Almeida, Arabic, and Niemeyer, German. I am thence, with satisfaction, a mestizo, as mestizos are all my Brazilian brothers.

It's easy to explain my concern on quoting that obstinately in the books I have been writing.

Things of the past. My youth lived in my grand parents, the Ribeiro de Almeida's house in Laranjeiras. Remembrances of those old times. The welfare we always had and him, for so many years as a Minister of the Supreme Court, dying poor and leaving to us, bonded, nothing but that house in Laranjeiras. Memories of a time of correction, not always followed today.

All these things explain my will of not leaving their name forgotten. The name of those who were so good for us all.

How things changed after my granddad's death!
Life became more difficult; my father's typography could not support new compromises and, little by little, the need of simplifying it. Dad stayed in Copacabana and my wife, my daughter, our cousin Milota and I moved to a modest house in Leblon.

I studied at the Fine Arts School. I didn't work. We lived by letting a house that Milota had downtown.

During the third academic year at school, most students used to look for an apprenticeship within the big building companies, what guaranteed not only good training but also a reasonable salary. But I didn't want to follow them. In spite of our difficult financial situation, I preferred to frequent gratuitously Lúcio Costa and Carlos Leão's atelier, where I was said to find the pathway to good architecture. And this decision proves that, even by that time, money questions didn't preoccupy me. I just wanted to be a good architect.

As a student, I could not collaborate effectively, but I could draw, and thus, little by little, I felt myself more and more useful to those good friends. By that time the building companies were given the important works. Architects used to deal with smaller buildings, residences, leisure clubs, etc. That's the reason for Lúcio Costa's excitement when Minister Gustavo Capanema invited him to design the Education and Health Ministry's headquarters in Rio.

Enthused, he let another office to better organise his staff: Carlos Leão, Afonso Eduardo Reidy, Jorge Moreira and Ernani Vasconcelos. Recently graduated, I continued as their assistant. It was in this occasion that, by Lúcio's indication, Capanema invited Le Corbusier, under the pretext of giving some lectures in Rio, to design the *Universidade de Mangueira*. Lúcio indicated me to help him as a drawer, and for 15 or 20 days I got the opportunity to know him deeper. Every afternoon he came to see the drawings I was working on; he appreciated my way of drawing. He even published my sketches in a book on his works, and a friendly atmosphere was established between us.

By that time Lúcio decided to show to Le Corbusier the designs he had made to the Ministry's headquarters. And Le Corbusier was radical, proposing a new project. Two, indeed. One for an imaginary site by the sea, another for the definitive terrain. Surprised, but generous as always, Lúcio gave up the work that interested him so much, accepting and endorsing Le Corbusier's design.

It was arranged that Lúcio would be in charge of the design's progress. And the drawing works began under the direction of Afonso Reidy and Jorge Moreira.

8

Personally I preferred Le Corbusier's first design, it was a lot more beautiful and, don't know why, I decided to make some sketches based on it. I put the main building in the centre of the terrain, made the auditorium and exhibition areas independent, creating an open air area that would allow people to pass through the building, from one side to the other.

Leão liked the sketches. Lúcio came and asked me to see the drawings but, not intending to interfere in the project, I threw them away through the window. Lúcio demanded someone to pick up the sketches downstairs and, enthused like Leão, he decided to adopt them.

The drawing works were in a very advanced stage then. I remember Jorge Moreira saying afflicted: "Lucio, the design is nearly ready!" But Lúcio was inflexible and my croquis were adopted.

It's obvious that my situation changed in view of what was going on. I became part of the architects' board and, gradually, the more listened and actuating one.

We always declared, and it is on the inauguration memorial tablet in that building, that it's a Le Corbusier's design, without giving emphasis to the modifications that we were obliged to do during the design process. But, nowadays, I can see that our collaboration was not that small. We put the main block in the centre of the terrain, what guaranteed free access to the exhibition room and the auditorium, through the large open space that, as I explained before, allows people to cross the building from one side to the other. And the high columns, which were hidden behind the glass panels, became then more imponent, like real pilotis. According to Le Corbusier`s design, all the external columns would be only four meters high. Inside the main block, we were obliged to make a central corridor, in substitution to the side gallery. The original project created a main façade and a secondary

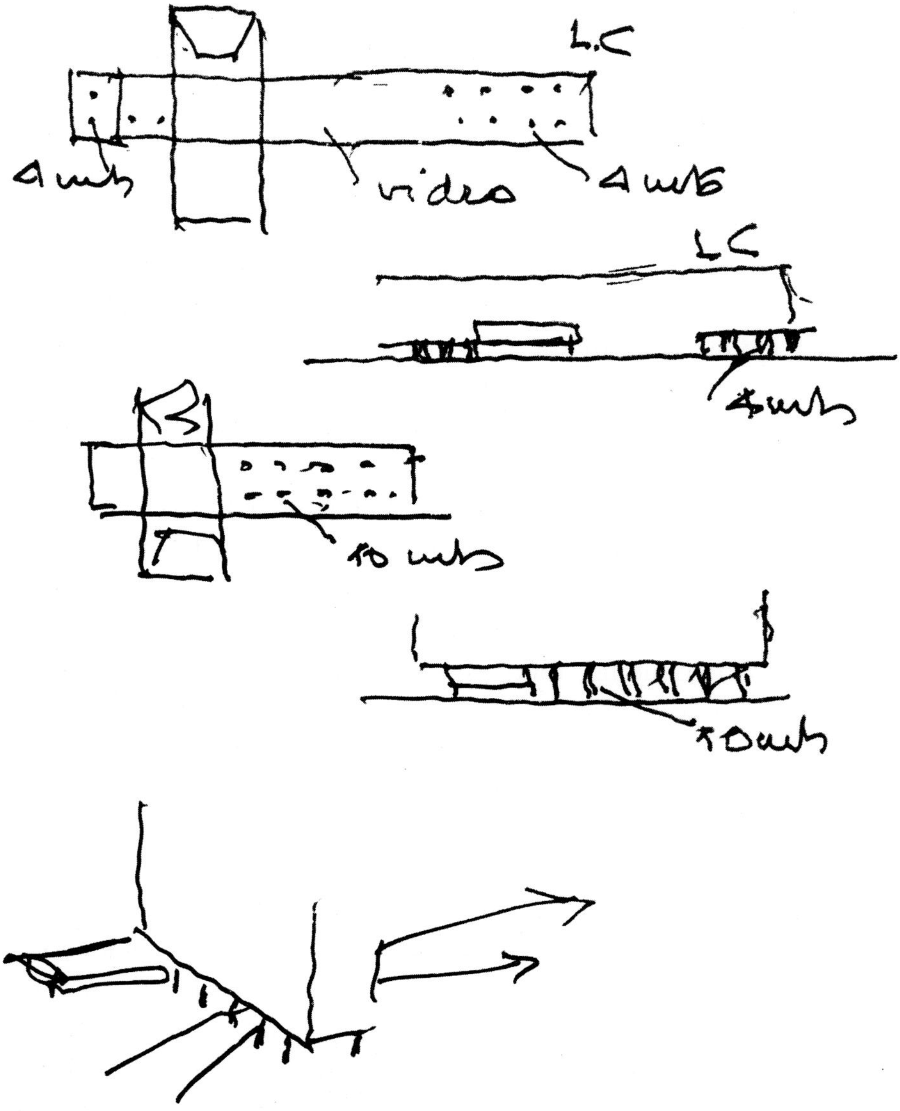
LC
video
LC

one, but, within the adopted solution, it was possible to make both similar, eliminating the salient blocks destined to the toilettes, which took the purity of the back façade. Regarding the *brise-soleils* , which Le Corbusier used to make in reinforced concrete, we preferred to make it movable, to better protect the interiors. These alterations, nearly all, were in the sketches that I presented. In my point of view however, little influence they had upon the importance of Le Corbusier`s design.

Still during Capanema's period, Lúcio did a new study for the *Universidade de Mangueira*. It was an important project. I remember the large perspectives that I drew in charcoal, and the sketches that I did on the walls, late at night.

I think he considered my actuation quite relevant. I remember him saying categorically by the end of the works: "Jorge, you can't earn more than Oscar. You must add your salaries and divide it in two". And my intervention was: "I propose adding the three salaries, Jorge's, Reis' and mine, and divide it into three". Reis earned the same I did.

It was not the first time that Lúcio supported me. In 1937, winner of the New York Pavilion design competition, he appreciated the design that I presented, and insisted on taking me to the United States.

~

Sometimes it happens that a minor incident has a major influence upon our lives. That's what made Capanema and I life-long friends.

During the construction of the ministry's headquarters, Capanema designated Carlos Leão to organise the university's project, under the direction of former minister Souza Campos. Yet counting on the collaboration of Reidy and Jorge Moreira, Leão convoked me: "Oscar, I want you to design the hospital but, if Souza Campos asks you which building you are designing,

11

don't tell him it's the hospital. He is a complete cretin and wants every hospital to be 'Y' shaped." A few days later the former minister came up to my drawing board and asked me: "Which building is this?" It was impossible to lie and I said: "It's the hospital." Angry, he punched the table: "I don't want these sausage-shaped things here!" That's how he defined the linear block that Le Corbusier had designed for that ministry's headquarters.

We argued. I said everything he should be said and sent in my resignation. Capanema refused it and convoked me to his office, where I stayed, helping him on everything related to architecture and arts. And we became good friends. It was Capanema who introduced me to Governor Benedito Valadares and, after, to Juscelino Kubitschek, who would come to have so much influence upon my architect's career.

I learned a lesson then. Sometimes it is necessary to say no. And even if we loose in the present, we still may have benefits in the future. That day, if I hadn't said no, Capanema wouldn't have approached me and consequently, I wouldn't have designed Pampulha and Brasilia.

Capanema was then no longer just the understanding minister who always distinguished us, but a real fraternal friend that, even after leaving the ministry, as a Republic's Senator then, always reclaimed my presence, pleased to see me around, to chat and remind those old times.

Capanema's actuation as the Minister of Education was so correct and idealistic that, even being this an architectural book, I shall say some words about him. To remind that it was Capanema who created the National Historic and Artistic Patrimony's Service – the SPHAN, which, conducted by Rodrigo M.F. de Andrade, put an end to the pillage routine that degraded our churches and old monuments.

A couple of years ago, my friend, poet Ferreira Gullar, then Funarte's president (National Arts Foundation), organised an exhibition on my work, on the first floor of the Education and Health [nowadays, Education and Culture] Ministry building. But when they decided to occupy definitively that floor, I interceded and asked my friend Glauco Campello, IPHAN's president [Artistic and Historical Patrimony National Institute] to remove my exhibition and dedicate the entire floor to Capanema's life work. And regarding that building's design authorship, I suggested them to show Le Corbusier's studies, limiting our actuation to the modifications made by Lúcio Costa's team. Moreover, I suggested the SPHAN and Rodrigo M. F. de Andrade, who dedicated all his life to it, to be remembered. These are remaining memories of those old times, and that work now known as Palácio Gustavo Capanema, name that I suggested to Marco Maciel, then the Minister of Education, who replied me: "The homage makes justice to whom made the realisation of this magnificent work possible, an unique moment of creative freedom manifestation."

But, if I quote Capanema, for the same reasons I have to remember Rodrigo, to whom I owe my interest for reading and for the everyday subjects, always so much linked to architecture. He was the one to invite me to work at SPHAN, what ended up making me better understand our old architecture, the baroque churches, the old farm houses, the Columbandê Farm – the most beautiful of all, all whitewashed, with its spread roof, its wide verandas, so simple and respectable as all those old residences were. Together we walked by Ouro Preto, Congonhas, Sabará and these old cities anguished him so much. I remember the meetings organised by Rodrigo at SPHAN, with the presence of [his friends and eminent intellectuals] Mário de Andrade, Prudente de Morais Neto, Augusto Meyer, Lúcio Costa, and Afonso Arinos among others. And just now I can realise the

13

lessons I took then. I really remind him as a dear master, one of the most honest persons I have ever met.

The first important modern work, elaborated by a Brazilian architect was, as far as I remember, the ABI [Brazilian Press Association] headquarters, designed by the [Maurício and Marcelo] Roberto brothers.

It's obvious that, after my unexpected actuation on the Ministry headquarters' design process, I felt more optimistic about my capabilities for intervening properly on architecture. And it explains my liveliness while designing Pampulha, even being that the first important work that came onto my hands.

From Le Corbusier I used to remember the brilliant works he published, his texts, words that defined so well his ideas about architecture and urbanism. But I drove myself towards a freer, lighter architecture, graceful enough to better approach our old colonial churches, avoiding the more robust structures that he used to adopt. I remember the poem he once wrote about the right angle, so different from the one I did about the curve in my architecture:

"It's not the right angle that attracts me
Nor the hard, inflexible, straight line,
Created by man.
It's the free and sensual curve that seduces me,
The curve that I can see in the mountains of my country,
In the sinuous curse of its rivers,
On the sea waves,
On the body of the favourite woman.
The universe is all made of curves,
Einstein's curved universe."

Le Corbusier said once that I had Rio's mountains in my eyes. I laughed. I prefer to think like Andre Malraux, who said: "I keep inside myself, in my private museum, everything I have seen and loved in my life."

While designing Pampulha, I penetrated into this fascinating world of curves and unusual forms offered by the reinforced concrete.

Many times I was obliged to work under utmost urgency regime and fixed terms. I remember my first meeting with Juscelino Kubitcheck, when he told me enthusiastic: "Niemeyer, you will design the district of Pampulha [in the city of Belo Horizonte]. A large development by the dam, with a casino, a church and a restaurant". And, just as optimistic as when he built up Brasilia twenty years later, he concluded: "I need the casino design for tomorrow!" And that is what I did, working all night long in a hotel in the city.

Pampulha was the beginning of Brasilia. The same enthusiasm, same rush. The same preoccupation on following the schedule. How happy JK was, taking us for a ride in a speedboat, late at night, just to show us the buildings' reflection on the dam's water!

17

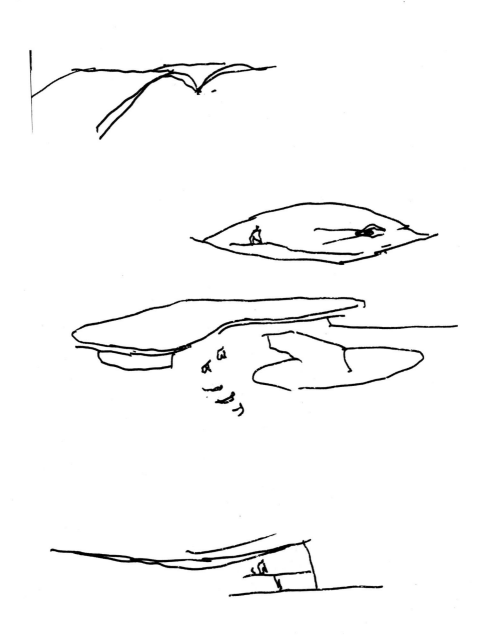

I did many trips to Pampulha, via Rio-Belo Horizonte road, and with great interest I accompanied the building works, together with my friend, engineer Marco Paulo Rabello, and in a short time they were concluded, modern and unusual, as we pretended them to be. I remember the casino in operation; the walls dressed up with onyx, the aluminium columns, and the city's *beau monde* showing off themselves on the ramps to the gambling room and the club. It was the sophisticate and festive ambient that JK wished. And the church, covered by curves, enriched by Portinari's mural and *via sacra*, Ceschiatti's low relieves and Paulo Werneck's drawings on the covering. I liked, over all, the main façade, covered by the huge Portinari's wall tiles panel.

When designing the club, JK advised me smiling: "[Governor] Benedito [Valadares] thinks that there are too many columns in the casino." But the drawings were already done, and the club is there, with its façade suggesting the internal solutions, leaning over the dam's waters.

It was in the *Casa do Baile* — the ball room — where I nimbly occupied myself with the curves, the marquee going alongside the island's limits, free and undulate as I wished.

In Pampulha my architecture's plastic vocabulary began to be defined, like an unexpected game of straight lines and curves. The great curved coverings coming down in straight lines, giving the coverings an unusual aspect that the structural thrust justified. Some other times the coverings unfolded themselves into unexpected and repeated curves, which my architect's imagination created.

And within this world of new and unknown forms, I was obliged to write down explanatory texts to go along with each project. When I designed, a blotting paper shaped auditorium, for a school in Belo Horizonte, I had to explain, in a supplementary text, that its shape was originated from the established visibility curves. When I designed my own residence in

19

Canoas [Rio de Janeiro], plenty of curves in its covering, I had to make clear that they followed the internal solution. Even regarding the "V-shaped" columns, which I once designed and that should not scare those who knew the Doges Palace in Venice, I had to explain that the different spans in the ground floor and its floors above suggested me that solution.

This need of better elucidating my designs drove me into a very particular working process. When I come to a solution, I describe it in an explanatory text. If after reading it satisfies me, I start the definitive drawings. If, otherwise, the arguments do not sound me reasonable, I return to my drawing board. It's like an acid test. Actually, in most of the cases, it's by reading the texts that I approve my designs. Few, very few people know architecture's secrets.

From Pampulha to Brasilia I did many designs. So many that I am going to occupy myself with just a few of them.

It pleases me, for example, to talk about the National Stadium of Maracanã [Rio de Janeiro], a solution that excited me then but which time made me see it in a different way.

By that time, the utmost idea regarding football stadiums was that the less sunned area should group the great majority of spectators. On the stalls in front – the sun-filled half of the stadium – we should put just a small percentage of the audience. This was the orientation that we adopted, and the design excited us with a huge 300-metre arch sustaining the great marquee's overhang. And all the complex, seven meters sunk down, to avoid suffocating the surrounding areas.

The commission short-listed two projects, ours inclusive, recommending that nothing should be designed for under the ground's natural level. But, advised by engineer Baumgarten, the most distinguished one by that time, we demanded a site sounding and, as we found compact argyle in quote –11, we contested that

commission. We went further down four meters and were eliminated, always thinking that our design was the best one.

Time passed and, assiduous football frequenters that we are, we ended up realising our equivocation. The important was, on the contrary, to keep the same public's density all over the stadium and, therefore, the festive atmosphere would multiply the widespread euphoria, propagating it throughout the whole stadium.

I remember a lecture in the Instituto dos Arquitetos do Brasil [Brazil's Architects Institute] and how surprised one of the winner project's authors was when I said that his design was better than ours.

What a mischief! Many years later, one evening in the ambassadress Maria Martins' Petropolis residence, her husband's friend, already deposed President Getúlio Vargas, who I had never met before, came up to me and said: "Dr. Niemeyer, if I were still in duty, your design for the National Stadium would have been built." I laughed, not saying a simple word, but willing to affirm: the other one was better.

It falls me to explain the design of the Ouro Preto Hotel, old city, the most important one of our colonial period. It was necessary to build up a new hotel in the city, and the SPHAN decided that the right path was a modern work that could mark the contrast between the new and the old architecture.

I designed it and, for the first time in our country, we built up duplex shells with bedrooms on the mezzanine, and, like reminiscences of the old times, latticework in the verandas and whitewashed walls, all in the good Portuguese tradition.

The hotel was poorly built, and I tried to recuperate it many times. One day the Governor of Minas Gerais State, Israel Pinheiro, commissioned me to design a huge building in Belo Horizonte. I did the job and sent him a letter asking him to destine my honorary to that hotel's recuperation. He appreciated the letter, hung it on the palace's wall and tried to actualise my request. But the person in charge of the repairs damaged even more what should be recuperated. It was just after the hotel's sale that a new owner took action. The pilotis void was emptied, the *grand salons* were repaired but the only shell, remade to the original design — was not multiplied as promised.

Some times the undesirable comes up. That`s what happened when Max Bill, passing by Rio, criticised Pampulha. Lúcio Costa wrote to the newspapers saying: "Without Pampulha, Pedregulho would not have been possible." From far away — how things propagate! — Alvar Aalto wrote me. "Niemeyer, today I put the last shovel over Mx Bill". And the little man returned to his insignificance.

~

In 1947, Wallace Harrison invited me to join the architects' team in charge of the United Nations' headquarters design. As soon as I arrived in New York, Le Corbusier called me up in the hotel demanding a meeting in one of the 5th Avenue's corners.

It was quite cold. Gentle, he put his coat over mine, saying: "I will do it like Saint Francisco". Since Oscar Nitzke's place was nearby, we walked up to it while he told me his story.

His design was being criticised and he wanted me to be by his side, collaborating on his project. And for a couple of days I tried to help him, but Wallace Harrison convoked me to his office: "Oscar, I invited you, like all the other architects, to present your own design, not to work with Le Corbusier." I told Le Corbusier about what had happened and he said: "You can't go, it will cause such a confusion." But, some days later, he advised me: "You would better go. They are waiting for your design."

I did my study in one week. I confess I didn't like Le Corbusier's design. I think it was done for another site, and the building for the Great Assembly and the Councils, in the centre of the terrain, would divide it in two.

In my design I kept the indispensable United Nation's block but I separated the Council Chambers from the General Assembly, placing the Chambers lower down, in a long building by the river and the General Assembly by the end of the terrain. And then, I had created the United Nations Square.

Budiansky, Le Corbusier's assessor, was the very first person to see my design. He said: "You did it better than Le Corbusier". Corbusier, who came soon after, examined it attentively and commented: "It's an elegant project!"

Wallace Harrison called me up once again: "Oscar, everybody prefers your project. I'll have to propose it in the next meeting".

By this meeting day I met China's representative architect in the lift, and he said: "Today I'll be by your side." In the beginning of the meeting Le Corbusier tried to defend his design: "I didn't make nice drawings, but it's the scientific solution for the United Nations' briefing". And I realised that he referred to my drawings.

The meeting began. Wallace Harrison proposed my design and it was accepted unanimously. They greeted me. Even the secretary came to hug me. My design was chosen.

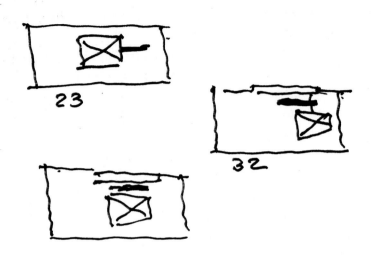

23

32

The day when Oscar Niemeyer's project 32, for the UN's headquarters, was unanimously chosen, in New York.

But, in the way out, Le Corbusier came and said: "I want to talk to you early tomorrow."

The other day, I came to see him. He wanted to move the General Assembly to the centre of the terrain: "Hierarchically it is the most important element, its place is there, in the centre", he said. I didn't agree. It would annihilate the United Nations Square, again dividing the terrain.

But Le Corbusier insisted. He seemed so concerned that I decided to accept it. And together we proposed a new study, the 23-32 project (23 was his project number and 32, mine).

Wallace Harrison didn't like my decision. After all, he had consulted me before.

The works continued. Slight modifications were made and, in reality, the building corresponds — and it's easy to verify, in it's volumes and free spaces — to the 23-32 project.

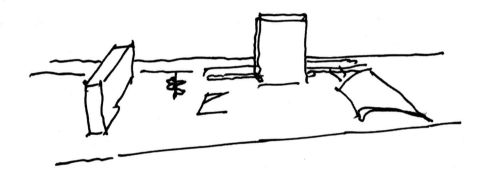

But I have to consider it as teamwork. Our task was to define the architectonic party. Wallace Harrison, Abramovitz and their collaborators did all the rest. From Harrison and Abramovitz I well remember their honesty and friendship.

Regarding Le Corbusier, he never mentioned the 23-32 project, but, I remember, months later, having lunch in his apartment, he looked at me and said: "You are generous." And I realised that, a bit late perhaps, he was remembering that morning in New York when, to be attentive to him, I put my design, the one that the Architects Commission had chosen, aside.

It would be natural, given the facts that I have just mentioned, if I had any bruise when talking about Le Corbusier. But I don't. I remember him, today, with the same enthusiasm that, 40 years ago we went to pick him up at the airport. The genial architect who seemed to come down from heaven that day.

Instead, I always remember him as a human being who brought us a message, a beauty chant that could not be silenced.

I'd rather stop by here. I have nothing else to say about what happened while we studied the United Nations project.

But it doesn't impede me to feel a bit sad, when I see the photo of the built complex. Oh... the United Nations Square that I designed is missing so much!

~

One day I went to Venezuela, to meet Inocencio Palacios, who wanted me to design a museum in Caracas. The site was beautiful, a plateau overlooking the city. I like this trip, the museum that I designed — an inverted pyramid, leaning towards the landscape. There I met Fruto Vivas, who collaborated with me, my friend until these days, one of the most competent and up to date architects I know.

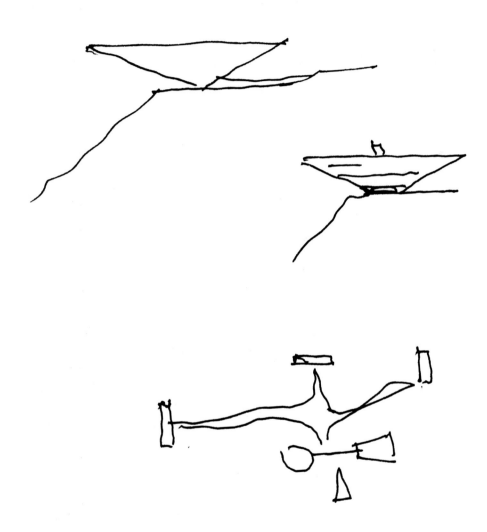

By this time, Orozimbo Loureiro and Otavio Frias commissioned me to make some works in São Paulo. Designs of real state's character that little influenced that city's architecture. My closer contact was with Frias who, courageously, decided to build up the COPAN building which, with its long and sinuous façade, constitutes, nowadays, a landmark of the Paulistan architecture.

By the occasion of São Paulo City Fourth Centenary, Ciccillo Matarazzo invited me to design the Ibirapuera Park. It was an important work, and I said that I would do it but not on my own. I called two local architects, Lotufo and Kneese de Melo and, together with Hélio Uchôa, from Rio, we did the project. Three large buildings for exhibitions, the monumental entrance with a museum and an auditorium, and a long marquee uniting the whole conjunct.

For years the entrance of the Ibirapuera Park was not completed, and the dome, originally destined for large exhibitions, was given to the [Ministry of] Air Force, for exhibiting air planes. And this equivocation, which took its scale away, made me forget it completely.

A few days ago, however, a group of idealist people, like Ricardo Ohtake , Edemar Cid Ferreira and Carlos Bratke, decided to recuperate it. Architect Paulo Mendes da Rocha, with special talent, renewed and updated it, declaring to the press that, it is "the most beautiful oca[1] in the world". Other people called me up, fancying this dome that I designed forty years ago, and that just now I got the opportunity to see it being used in its original purpose. A story, difficult to occur in an architect's life, which made me happy, thinking, for some moments, that the world is not that perverse, that there is still understanding and solidarity on it.

---

[1] Brazilian native Indians' traditional dwelling in the shape of a dome, made of a timber structure covered with a particular type of leaves.

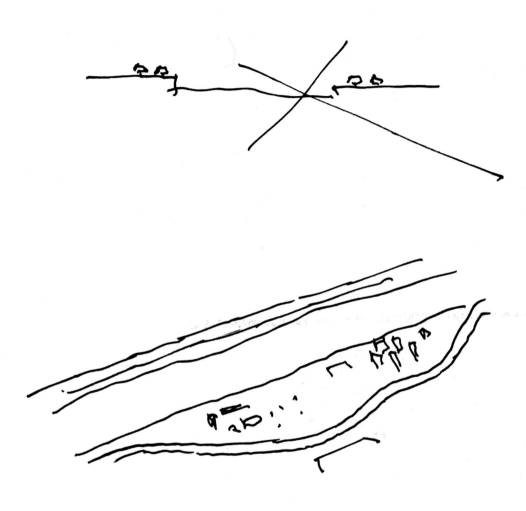

Another project in São Paulo, in the 80's, and I regret it was not taken forward, is the urbanisation of the Tietê riverbank side. The river is walled by two big avenues. Our proposal was to push one of the avenues a few kilometres away, in order to create an artificial beach.

The project was taken further, and Jânio[2] approved it. But then Erundina[3] came up: our project was filed and the Tietê keeps on running walled. It was the active insensibility following us.

During the long period in between Pampulha and Brasilia, I kept in contact with Juscelino Kubitscheck and, on his demand, I did a few projects for Minas Gerais State. In Belo Horizonte city, the Colégio Estadual [State's School], Júlia Kubitscheck School, the Banco Mineiro da Produção, the State's Library, the Municipal Theatre, and yet a resort for Diamantina city.

It was only in 1957 that the new capital problem came up. JK came to my residence in Canoas and together we went downtown. He wanted to build up Brasilia, a new capital for our country, and repeating what happened in Pampulha, he wanted my collaboration – mine and Marco Paulo Rabelo's who, like me, followed him from Pampulha until Brasilia's inauguration. With enthusiasm, JK told me that he had a modern city in mind. "The most beautiful in the world!", he said, with excitement.

And it was arranged that I should see Israel Pinheiro, who was in charge of the building works. I met Israel and he said: "I can only pay you as an officer. But, as the IAB (Brazil's Architects Institute) proposes, it would be possible to give you a commission on the buildings costs". And the word "commis-

---

[2] Jânio Quadros, Brazil's President and, later, São Paulo City mayor.
[3] Luíza Erundina, former São Paulo city mayor following Jânio's government.

sion", which I hate, made me refuse his offer, working and designing all Brasilia's palaces with a modest monthly salary.

Actually, during Brasilia's construction, with my office in Rio paralysed, I needed to sell a small apartment that I owned off Praça General Osório, in Rio. Later, when JK called me up and said – "Niemeyer I want you to design the headquarters in Brasilia for Banco do Brasil and Banco do Desenvolvimento Econômico, and want you to earn according to the IAB's chart" – I replied: "I can't, I'm an officer".

I accompanied JK on his first trip to the site. I remember General Lott, the Minister of War, asking me: "The Army's building will be modern or classics?" And I answering: "In a war, do you prefer modern weapons or the classic ones?" And he smiled with sympathy.

It was a three hours flight. I confess I did not have a good impression of the site. Far away from everything, it was an abandoned, empty land. But JK's enthusiasm was such, and the purpose of driving the progress inward was so valid that we all ended up agreeing with him.

The distance and the convenience of keeping JK in the premises, to keep the venture's vigour, made us realise that we should begin the works by building up an inn, where he could stay in the weekends. A wooden house was thought. I did the plans. Juca Chaves and Milton Prates organised the construction, and I signed a promissory note that, cashed from a bank, allowed us to build up this small building, known as "Catetinho". In fifteen days time JK was already using it. It was his refuge from the politics, from the ones who contested the construction of the new capital. It was where he used to chat with his friends, discussing how would that city be like, his favourite dream. Surrounding the small building, a group of trees – like a small oasis – distinguished it from the plain and empty land of the cerrado[4]. I remember that, the fresh water came from a reservoir, suspended on one of the trees; the chatting place was under the pilotis, on a long table with wooden benches. There was whisky and lots of comradeship. Early in the morning, our friend Bernardo Sayão brought the necessary provisions by helicopter, and Brasilia was in the heart of all of us yet.

The design works began in the the Ministry of Education and Health headquarters in Rio de Janeiro. Soon after, I realised the convenience of moving to Brasilia. And I proceeded with my collaborators. I didn't intend to bring only architects with me and so I invited other friends – a doctor, two journalists and four other comrades who were not into architecture – they were unemployed, intelligent and funny, and I realised that it would be a good moment to help them. Actually, I didn't want to spend the nights talking about architecture in Brasilia. For me, life is much more important , architecture is just a complement.

~

The Pilot Plan was an urgent problem, and we organised an international competition. Upset, JK proposed me: "Niemeyer, we cannot waste time. Do the Pilot Plan yourself". But I didn't accept it. I thought perhaps even Eduardo Reidy would participate in the competition. He was, among all of us, the most informed on the theme, even because of his job in Rio's Municipality. But it didn't happen. And Lúcio Costa came up with his exceptional talent.

I remember some people trying to cancel the competition, in its very end, when Lúcio's design was in evidence. IAB's president called up Israel Pinheiro, suggesting the nomination of a commission of urban planers to design a new project. Israel said that it was up to me, and it was in the Clube dos Marimbás [at Rio de Janeiro], in the presence of architect João Cavalcanti, that I declared: "From me, you will have all obstacles". And Lúcio was the winner.

---

[4] Native vegetation in Brazil's central region.

With architects and colleagues in Brasilia

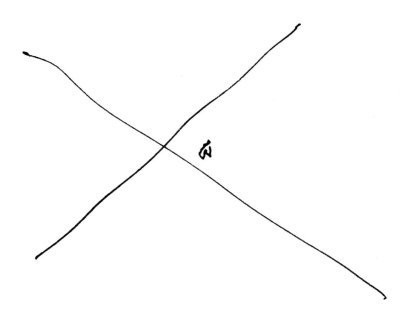

With Israel Pinheiro and Bernardo Sayao, on the outlook for a proper site to build up Alvorada Palace in Brasília.

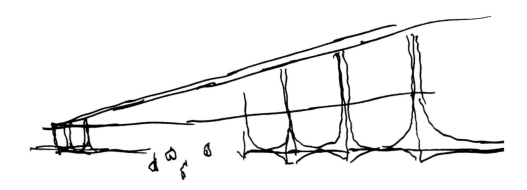

It was an innovative urban solution, with different independent sectors, the residential area linked to small shops and the schools; the Monumental Axis reminding the greatness of our country, and the Praça dos Três Poderes, (Tree Powers Square) finishing it and overlooking the cerrado, as he preferred.

And the plan developed itself within a varied scale. Sometimes human, sometimes monumental, like only a sensible man like Lúcio could conceive.

The first project to be initiated in Brasilia was the Alvorada Palace. Its location was not even fixed by the Pilot Plan yet, but we couldn't wait. And we went, Israel Pinheiro and I, looking for a proper site, grass hitting our knees, throughout the cerrado.

I did the project. A simple two storey building. It was the President's residence and his working area. With accuracy we designed both areas like interlacing yet keeping the desirable independence. And its wide veranda without parapet, one meter above the ground level, protected by a row of columns that succeeded one another in repeated curves. I remember André Malraux visiting the palace: "These are the most beautiful columns I have ever seen after the Greek columns" – he said. And they were copied in Brazil, in a post office building in the United States, in Greece, Libya, everywhere. It didn't bother me. Like in Pampulha, I accepted it gratified. It was a proof that many people do like my work.

This palace suggested things of the past. The façade's horizontal direction, the wide veranda protecting the building, even the little chapel by the edge of the composition, reminding our old farm houses.

After Alvorada Palace, we began the study of the Monumental Axe and started our project by Praça dos Três Poderes. It should be composed, according to the pilot plan, by Palácio

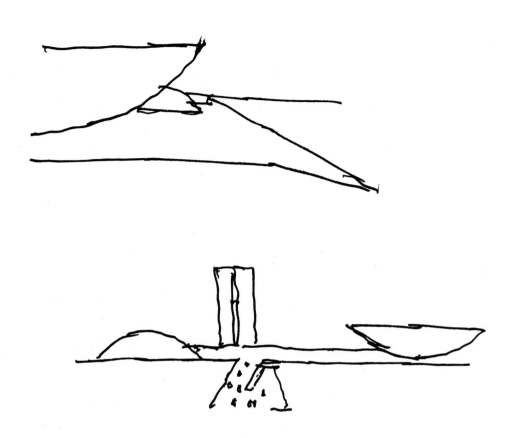

do Planalto, the Supremo Tribunal Federal and the Congress — the latest positioned a bit far off. A distance that ponds and palm trees rows seemed to justify.

But the idea of integrating the Congress within the square preoccupied me, and it explains the fact that I kept the palace's top on the avenues level, allowing the visitor who approximates it to overlook, in between the projected domes, the square that the palace is part of.

This solution made the Senate's and Chamber's domes more imponent, monumental, exalting the hierarchic importance that they represent in the conjunct. I remember Le Corbusier saying to Ítalo Campofiorito while going up the Congress ramp: "There is invention here!" The huge domes of that palace surprised him for the inventive audacity that it exhibited.

While designing Palácio do Planalto and Palácio do Supremo, I decided to keep them into more regular forms. The key element of plastic unity would be the supports. That explains the freer design that I adopted for the columns in these two buildings, and the palaces like just touching the ground. An architectonic solution that Joaquim Cardozo, engineer and poet, the more cultured Brazilian I've ever met, defended. "One day I will make them even finer, in solid steel" – he said.

The drawing on the page besides shows, in a cut of Palácio do Planalto, the type of structure that I designed, richer, undoubtedly, than the one a less audacious architecture would have preferred.

For the two next buildings, Palácio da Justiça [Ministry of Justice] and the Itamaraty [Ministry of Foreign Policy], my idea was to foresee a simpler architecture, this elegant and repetitive one that we can see everywhere around. Easy to be elaborated and accepted by the great majority.

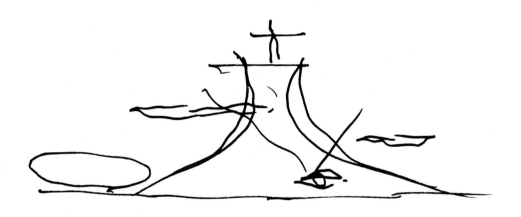

It would be kind of a pause, a moment of reflection for better understanding the freer architecture that I prefer.

The idea of making a different architecture allows me to affirm nowadays to those visiting the new capital: "You will see the palaces of Brasilia, you may like it or not, but may never say you have seen something similar before". This is the case of Brasilia's Cathedral. Different from all cathedrals in the world, an expression of the reinforced concrete and the pre-fabricated technique. Its columns were filled with concrete on the floor, for creating the architectural spectacle afterwards. A dedicated work that architect Carlos Magalhães da Silveira conducted with plenty of competency. And it's worthy remembering other details, enriching the architecture like the lighting contrasts, the shadowed gallery and the coloured nave. And Marianne Peretti's beautiful stained glasses, Ceschiatti's angels, and the unique possibility, that once enchanted one of the Pope's representatives, for the believers to look through the transparent glass, watching the infinite space, where they believe the Lord to be. It's the architect inventing his architecture, which few, very few people will be able to understand.

By the other side of the Monumental Axis there are the theatres. Two theatres that complete themselves in a pyramidal shape. It's an attractive building, with a huge gardened hall, covered with glass, and a rooftop restaurant, overlooking the landscape.

For many years the conclusion of the axis has been postponed, and just now the dream of seeing it finished is about to come true. But this is a subject that I will treat afterwards, when commenting my latest works.

It was not easy to work in Brasilia, and the design for the National Congress building is a good example. A design elaborated without a briefing, without any idea on how the number of members of the parliament would multiply in the future. All-in-a-

15

hurry was the word of command. I remember how we began that project. Israel Pinheiro and I went to Rio in order to measure the old Congress in that city, to multiply its area and its existing sectors and then beginning the drawings.

That's what explains the supplementary buildings and the political problems that occurred later. Mentioning one of them will be enough to give a feel of our difficulties. When the Parliamentarism came up, the great hall of the Congress was occupied by new rooms and cabinets, what demanded an urgent solution. That hall was indispensable and those rooms should be close to the plenary. I wanted to defend the palace's architecture, and the solution was to enlarge its width in 15 meters. The views to the square, that we could overlook from the old salon, were lost, but the external architecture of the palace was preserved with such accuracy that no one realises its modification, which as an architect, I will always regret.

Happily, the contact with deputies and senators was so cordial and the actuation of my friend Luciano Brandão, general secretary [of the Chamber of Deputies] then, was so skilled that the works in the Congress followed without problems.

Recently, I designed three new buildings for Brasilia — the Procuradoria Geral da República [House of the State's Procurators] and the supplementary buildings for the Supremo [Supreme Court] and the Tribunal de Contas da União [The Union`s Audit Court]. Buildings, in my view, of relevant architectonic importance but, for some, of excessively expensive construction. I remember how much I defended these buildings. They are public buildings, I know that my poorer brothers will not use them, but if the buildings are beautiful and different, they will stop and watch them, and it will be a moment of surprise and enchantment for them.

~

Like life itself, Brasilia has got good and bad moments. One of the best, so good it even reminded me the JK period, was with governor José Aparecido de Oliveira. He built up the The Liberty

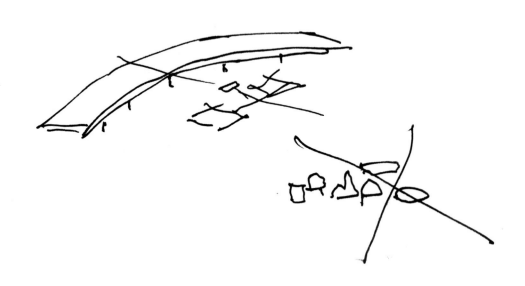

Pantheon,[5] he finished the Cathedral, the Praça dos Três Poderes and built up, on my demand, Lúcio Costa`s Memorial. It was this friend of mine who tried to improve the [Brasília's] satellite-cities, making them more welcoming and, thus defending the Pilot Plan from the demographic explosion.

Another period that I remember impassioned is that when, with great effort, Darcy Ribeiro succeeded to create the University [of Brasília]. We designed it in a extensive building alone, 600 meters long. It was the *Minhocão*, (Big Worm) as he used to nickname it. He appreciated so much this solution that, before leaving the University, he made a point of finishing the whole structure.

Unhappily, until we left the University, only the small School of Architecture had been concluded – a ground level building with internal patios and murals that I myself did on its walls. João Filgueiras Lima (our *Lelé*), Glauco Campello, Ítalo Campofiorito, Carlos Bittencourt among others, also took part in the architecture school.

~

One of the trips I did abroad was to Lebanon, where I was commissioned to design a huge international exhibition. And it was in Tripoli that I did my job during one month. I remember Beirut, where I used to spend the weekends, a city said to be the "Mediterranean pearl" – the street from Tripoli to Beirut; the small settlement said to be one of the oldest cities in the world, with its small theatre in ruins by the sea, some streets still there, and funerary vases lying about. And there we stood still, imagining how would have lived our ancestors, a primitive life, defenceless, but with the same desires and inquietude that still afflict us. I loved that hotel in Beirut, its large terrace overlooking the Mediterranean, the conversations among friends, talking about life and architecture.

––––––––––––––––––

[5] Memorial building in homage of Brazilian former politics leaders.

While studying this project, I didn't want to repeat the usual international exhibitions of that time (like the New York one, for example) — with its independent pavilions of so bad architecture and confusing structures that I hate. And I designed a huge long block where the countries would make their exhibitions. Architecture would be simpler, disciplined. An open-air auditorium and the Lebanon Museum would enrich the conjunct.

The construction began, the structures were concluded but the complex is still unfinished, due to the wave of violence that took the country. Today I met my cousin Camargo who, together with Dimanche, collaborated with me on that project. What an architectural lesson lost in time!

~

1964. I was leaving to Europe, Paris. Darcy Ribeiro, Head of the Presidency's Civil Cabinet, said enthusiastically during my farewell: "Oscar we are at power!" And there was a certain reason for that: João Goulart's government was hand in hand with the most progressive forces in our country. But it was in Lisbon, two months later, that I listened perplexed from a radio in the hotel the news that the militaries had taken the power. It was the military *coup d'État* that for twenty years suffocated the Brazilian people.

I stayed some months in Europe. When I came back to Brazil, I was taken to an Army headquarter, the day after my arrival, to testify. Two friends waited outside to know what would happen to me. Nothing important. The same old questions: Cuba, Moscow, etc.

It was not the first time it happened to me. The social problem, the misery that multiplies in our country, these things always prevailed in my preoccupations. Still young, in my 20's, I used to help the Socorro Vermelho (Red Aid) and, when in 1945

Prestes[6] came out of prison, where he stayed secluded, incommunicable for nine years, I decided to help him, welcoming in my office one dozen of communists who had come out of prison with him. One day – I never forget – I said to Prestes: "Keep this house for you, your task is more important than mine". And my office was transformed into the headquarters of the Brazilian Communist Party's Metropolitan Committee.

Since my youth until today, the political struggle has always occupied me. It's more important for me than the sixty years that I have spent on the drawing board.

In my professional contacts I never hide my political positions. Most people who like my architecture think I am equivocate; I think the same of them.

When we began to built Brasilia, I was convoked by the political police, and I told JK what was going on: "You can't go" – he said. "They will take your picture and I won't be able to see you in the palace". By telephone, he talked to the police chief in my presence: "Niemeyer can't go. He is a key element for Brasilia's construction".

Months later, I had to go. They took me to a sound proof compartment and after the usual questions the policeman asked me: "What do you communists aim for?" "Changing the society" – I answered. "Write down there" – said the policeman to a little black young man who tapped my declarations in a machine: "Changing the society". And this poor young man, looking at me exclaimed: "It will be difficult!"

And within this atmosphere of violence and ignorance we lived for a long time in our country. And if the freedom of expression was recuperated, it is intrinsically a decoy used by the reactionary forces to impose themselves upon the unprepared people.

---

[6] Luís Carlos Prestes, Brazilian most known communist leader.

What mostly upsets me, apart from the misery, the unemployment, and the violence, is this pressure practised by the United States' government, not only on Latin American countries but also on all those countries that rise up against it.

For twenty years I have been refused a visa to enter the United States. I remember one day, being in Rome, I was invited to design a building in Miami, so I applied for this document at the North American consulate in that city. "This is impossible" – said the young lady who attended me. "Is it personal?", I asked. "Yes", she answered, and I said smiling: "You know, I feel happy for that. If even after 20 years you insist on refusing me this visa, this is an evidence that I am still the same person".

I could go further on other episodes, if this was not an architectural book. But, defending my political believes, the more modest they may be, seems necessary to me sometimes.

∼

Brasilia still worried me, forcing me to join the projects under execution, but little by little, after the military *coup d'État,* I felt the political pressure against me was becoming bigger and bigger. Air Force Minister declared to the press: "The place for communist architects is in Moscow", and the project I did for the Brasilia's airport was discontinued. The solution that I proposed – circular –, adopted afterwards in Paris' airport, was disapproved. Linear was the imposed solution. Dialog was impossible. We moved a legal action against the Air Force, which was conveniently denied by a judge from Minas Gerais.

But it was not only professionally that they tried to hit me. I remember my beloved house in Mendes, and the day when the construction of a new road nearby caused the overflow of a small river in the vicinity, destroying the house. Would it be a premeditate action? I don't know, but some notice, a forewarning at least, would have been indispensable.

Another violence, not only against me but also against the former-president JK, was the demolition of Julia Kubitscheck School, which I had designed. Another road ostensibly built towards it. And that work, which I had done with such a pleasure in homage of the former president's mother, disappeared forever.

As the situation degraded more and more, I decided to leave, and go to the "Old World", to disseminate my architecture. And those who intended to shut my mouth gave me, by accident, this opportunity.

~

One of the reasons why I decided to write this book is to explain the projects I did abroad. And it justifies the simple didactic way in which I shall approach them.

On my travels abroad, France was the first country I visited, and André Malraux was the one who helped me most. It was him who got directly from De Gaulle a work permit allowing me to work in the country, like a French architect.

I had been to Paris before, to the Champs Elysées, the Seine, the Rive Gauche, which I knew, from the books, to be the artists and intellectuals' favourite area in the old times. And the struggle for freedom and equality, revindication that has been marking this people's feeling.

As an architect, it pleases me the way they kept the architectonic unity in Paris, the six storey pattern, the high windows being repeated everywhere. And specially, the way they avoided the skyscrapers, leaving it to La Defense, where, provided the necessary space, they are being built.

But it was with my friends in the French Communist Party, Marchais, Leroy, Gosnat and Tricot, that I had a closer contact. I owe them the convocation to make the studies for the French Communist Party`s headquarters, the job centre building in Bo

With Georges Marchais and other members of the
French Communist Party in Paris.

bigny and the "Space Oscar Niemeyer" in Le Havre. The commission for the urbanisation of Grasse I owe to Malraux. I will detain myself on these works and on the Sainte-Baume's Covent.

Designing the headquarters for the French Communist Party, at Colonel Fabien Square, in Paris, with the collaboration of Jean Prouvé, Jean De Roche and Chemetov, was my first task. I started this project by locating the main block according to the terrain and the accesses, what justifies the adopted curve. Then I put the Workers Class' Great Salon, in the underground, what allowed the dome to not occupying the terrain more than necessary. It is the relation between volumes and open spaces, so many times forgotten, that I respected. The rest is the internal removable partitions, the beautiful window frames designed by my friend Jean Prouvé. And the adopted architecture was so logic and functional that, years later, willing to build up the headquarters for *L'Humanité* newspaper, the French Communist Party came back to me.

On its turn, the project for the Job Centre in Bobigny demanded a cheaper solution. Shorter spans, simpler and modulated window frames and removable internal walls. Only in the auditorium I allowed myself some fantasy, in the form adopted: a contrast to the simplicity of the main block that the architecture required, not increasing the construction costs.

The Space Oscar Niemeyer, in Le Havre, is kind of a huge square overlooking the sea. Surrounding it, Perret's severe architecture. I didn't want to create a strong contrast to that architecture, and since the briefing — theatre, cultural centres — foresaw buildings with few openings, I did them nearly "blind", like huge abstract sculptures. All in consonance with its interior conveniences.

I began this project demanding them to lower the square down four meters. Therewith I wanted not only to protect it from

the cold sea breeze but also to allow people to see it from a higher level. It is – I believe – the only square of this kind in Europe.

It pleases me to remember this work that occupied me a lot, and the day when my friend Massimo Gennari – a brilliant architectural professor who collaborated with me in the FATA headquarters in Turin – called me up to say: "Oscar, Bruno Zevi declared that he would classify your work in Le Havre as one of the contemporary architecture's top ten examples".

~

One day the Dominicans from Sainte-Baume sought after me. They wanted me to design a complex of sleeping rooms, chapel, meeting spaces. They talked about ancient things, quiet ancient indeed, natural dwellings where the Christian religion appeared. And it took me to such a particular architecture that it's worthy remembering. Firstly, we would make the volumes we wanted of ground; then, we would cover them with a concrete slab. After removing the ground, the construction would be concluded. This development, which the drawings besides can better explain, was designed under this principle.

I also did Grasse's urbanisation project. A mountainous country overlooking a vast valley. So beautiful! I couldn't propose small isolated buildings, the views would disapear. One obstructing the others' view, and occupying too much the terrain. The idea was to create only three long apartment buildings, preserving the landscape, and a wide avenue connecting them to a square where we would locate the train station, administrative buildings, shops, theatre, cinemas, etc. This solution pleased me pretty much. I would like to see this development constructed. But the real states' men thought differently. They preferred small blocks, easier to build up and to sell out, what I couldn't accept. And the urbanisation of Grasse, which I designed with such cherish, remains on the paper.

I like Italy very much. The talent of our Italian co-leagues... How much surprised I was in front of the Doges Palace, designed by Candelario in Venice, like announcing the architecture of nowadays. The same search for beauty and architectural lightness, with its arches being multiplied on the floors above, avoiding supports, willing, like us, to conquer the free spaces – what he achieved beautifully in the great saloon, with a simple wodden trestlework.

Editor Giorgio Mondadori, who I didn't know, came to see me in Rio. He had been to Brasilia, loved the Itamaraty building, and wanted to build up his new headquarters in Milan, with a similar range of columns.

I said yes, but adopted solution was another one. After the arguments that follow, you will realise how different these two buildings are. It's the contrast that I mentioned before, between a correct and repeated architecture and another devoted to a more refined technique and to the architectural invention.

While the Itamaraty's columns, supporting only thecovering, had a section of only 70 X 25cm, in the Mondadori building columns – on which the roof beams and the five storey building were supported – the sections adopted were much bigger – 250 X 70 cm.

Thinking architecture as invention, I tried to give the range of columns of Mondadori building a distinctive rhythm. I wanted to run away from the always established uniform voids. I thought the proportion, the precise space between the columns, was as important as the columns themselves. I remembered Rilke saying: "How magnificent the trees are, but even more magnificent is the sublime and pathetic space in between them." And the Mondadori building was then built up, generating surprises, since, as far as I know, similar solution has never been

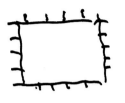

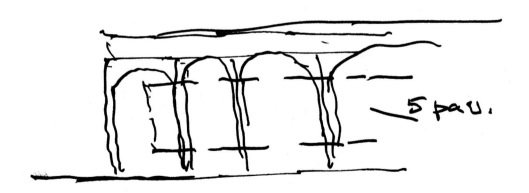

5 pav.

adopted before. Internally, the open plan that we prefer. And the headquarters works so well that, willing to edify another building in central Milan, Giorgio Mondadori commissioned me again.

I read this explanation, look on the sketches on the page besides and realise that this project, so well developed by Glauco Campello, attended all the reasons of a good architecture. Its volume corresponds to its briefing. It adopts the most modern technique, it's different from all other buildings of its kind, and for that very reason it contests the pejorative nomination – that to some people occur and to other buildings is extended, of *monumental building*. Monumental – it may well be – but in a good sense.

Oh, how great the old masters were, the ones who created the huge domes, the spectacular *voûtes*, and the great cathedrals! It is from them, monumental for sure, that architecture evolved.

Le Corbusier... How life confirms the value of intuition ! As a drawer at Perret s office, perhaps having never attended a technical school, one day he went his way throughout the Orient, thinking over his architecture. This talented architecture that mediocrity has criticised so much.

I have just received a pack from Milan, which has been sent to me by the current owners of that building. Beautiful photos by Gabriele Basilico, who is currently said to be one of the best Italian architectural photographers; a new video about the building and a letter, where they say with satisfaction that the building, designed so many years ago, keeps on being daily visited by architecture professors and students.

But this conviction, this enthusiasm with which I defend a palace like Mondadori's, doesn't prevent me from occupying myself, the same earnest way, with smaller projects.

I remember Le Corbusier, who said we shouldn't be afraid of the monumental, and how he dedicated himself, with

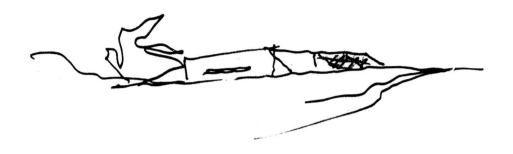

the same cherish, to a more modest project – his little house outside Paris for example, publishing the drawings he did for it. It happened to me many times – in my little house in Mendes and in the small chapel that I designed for a friend.

The site that I chose for this house in Mendes was outside the city, beautiful, with a little waterway separating the terrain from the road. There was a chicken roost previously built by masonry on it – 15 meters long and six meters wide and I decided to transform it into a little house. In one-month time it was ready. Simple, with its cement flooring, well integrated within the gardens, with a creeping plant full of flowers climbing the veranda's trestlework. I liked this house, its singleness, simplicity, so small that inside it I could feel better, like more protected.

Regarding the little chapel that I did to my friend, it may astonish you but, in truth, I designed that small chapel with the same care I did the big projects that came onto my hands. I was concerned to its good integration within the gardens, with the old existing residence, the pale pink colour of its walls. I even did the drawings of the Catholic saints in its interior. All that counted in the simple form of this little chapel. But it was missing something that could characterise it, something that could make it different. And I detained myself on its covering. Today, when someone passes by, in the dark nights of that huge garden, just the curves of its covering can be seen, like floating in the air, mysteriously. This is a small detail that pleases me very much in this project. Actually, it pleases me and my friend José Aparecido de Oliveira, its owner, who takes his friends to the garden in the evenings, just to see that unusual and unexpected light effect.

~

Still on my trip to Italy, I have to say some words about FATA headquarters, my friend Di Rosa – who has given me so much attention – about Turim, where I designed the building with the

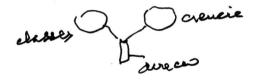

classes   creucie

sureca

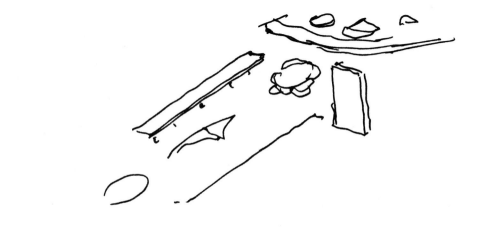

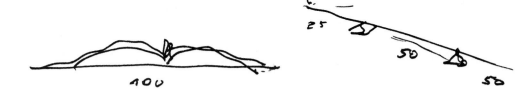

100

25

50

50

collaboration of my friend Massimo Gennari. Its structure was so accurate that Riccardo Morandi, the great Italian engineer who calculated it, declared in one of his books: "It was the first engineering work that forced me to have recourse to everything I knew on reinforced concrete." It demonstrates that, with my architects' fantasies, I contribute, the less it can be, to the evolution of the constructive technique. That is what my friend Lionello Puppi says in his book about my work.

~

My trip to Algeria ended up being extended to other countries in the Arabic world. But it was in Alger and Constantine where I stayed longer. I like the Algerian people very much, the happiness they manifested on the triumph of President Boumedienne's revolution. And Casbáh, with its curvaceous streets, all white, overlooking the Mediterranean. From my friends Dejelloul, Benyahiá, Guedehi, Berehi and Uldeniá, I keep good remembrances.

The project for the University of Constantine attracted us. We felt that it was time to realise Darcy Ribeiro's concept of "open university", that we had begun in Brasilia, but that was soon degraded after the military *coup d'État* in 1964. We convoked Darcy, anthropologist and educator; Heron de Alencar, literature teacher, Luís Hildebrando Pereira da Silva, biologist; Ubirajara Brito, nuclear physician; and we met and discussed with the local teachers. And our idea prevailed.

The briefing foresaw twenty buildings. We reduced it into six. The two-storey, 300 meters long "Classes Building" would house the classrooms and auditoriums. The "Sciences Building", with identical dimensions, would house the laboratories. And we would have a Library, the Auditorium, a restaurant and the administration high building. The solution adopted would allow

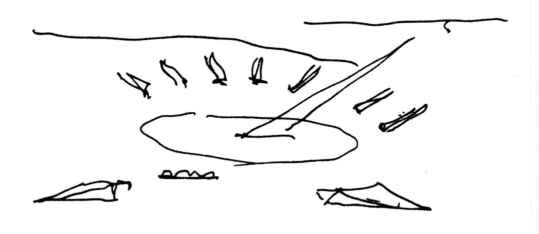

the creation of any new faculty, using the Classes and Sciences buildings. And it guaranteed the square an indispensable scale, distinguishing it, with its white and monumental architecture, from the dramatic landscape of Constantine.

After finishing the designs, we sent them to the technical bureau where they should be approved. The Classes Building surprised everybody, with its 50 meters long spans and 25 meters balance. They appreciated the solution advising us, carefully: "The walls supported by the columns will be 150 centimetres in width." And we did them with 30 centimetres.

Similar thing happened in the auditorium that we designed with an external beam and the covering wings touching the floor. Satisfied, engineer Bruno Contarini, who calculated the buildings said: "It's one more world record."

Another project engaged us in Algeria. The Alger Civic Centre, with all its palaces. A solution that pleased us, distributed like a fan, in front of the sea. The foundations were initiated but the accident involving our friend [Minister] Dejelloul stopped the construction. It was an impressive conjunct.

I also remember the monument that Boumedienne demanded us: a 300 meters long lance, pointing west.

Sometimes, when beginning a new design, an idea comes up to us naturally. That's what happened to the Alger mosque. I was in a hotel in that city, already in bed, thinking on the mosque, when an idea came up suddenly. And, like on a drawing board, I kept on imagining it. The curvaceous form, ascendant, the columns surrounding it and the hypothesis that it could be built up on the sea, by the beach, excited me a lot. I stood up, did the drawings and the indispensable connection between the mosque and the continent.

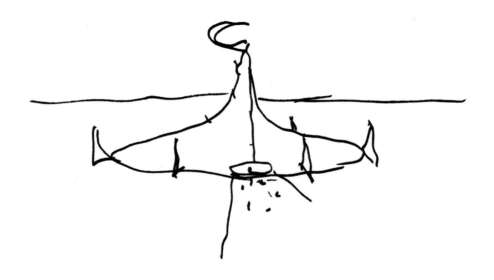

It would be a different mosque. When president Boumedienne saw it, he said: "But this is a revolutionary mosque!" And I went: "The revolution must not stop, Mr. President".

~

I did just a few works for the real states' market – apartment buildings, residences, and so on, always limited by money problems and bad taste. In compensation, working on public buildings, I engaged myself with several different architectural subjects.

Within all these projects, from time to time, I was always surprised by those really unexpected ones.

This is the case of the resort that I designed for an island in Abu Dhabi, Arab Emirates, and the small zoo in Algeria.

Regarding the resort, the briefing foresaw theatres, cinemas, museums, gymnasiums, swimming pools, etc. No vehicle would run in the island, which should be entirely dedicated to the pedestrians. The access was by maritime ways and only the personnel in charge of maintenance would live in the island.

According to my design, a monorail would cross longitudinally the island, with predetermined stops.

I see the photos and regret it hasn't been built. The program was such an assorted one that all the fantasies that architecture can possibly allows were offered me.

Regarding the zoo, my main idea was to keep the animals not jailed but free, like nature created them. Visitors would walk in a suspended glazed catwalk.

The walk would begin by visitors overlooking the large area destined to earth animals. Then, penetrating a huge aviary, varied birds flying around them. In the end, this catwalk would dive into a huge swimming pool; it would be the water world, the sea animals, inviting them to a further cognisance.

67

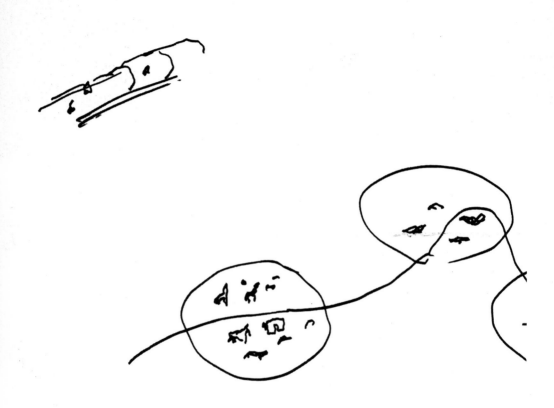

~

It's just about Alger University that I don't like to talk, despite the dedication of my friend Claudio Queiroz on this work.

Everything started in a bad way. Our idea was not accepted, and the project's most concise solution was lost.

The important however is that the Constantine University was built. It is one of my works abroad that mostly pleases me, despite of the distances, all the problems and the anguish faced by our friend Luís Marçal, who dedicated several years to this work.

~

One day I travelled to Israel, invited by X. Federmann to design a huge building in Tel Aviv. A welcoming city. The Israeli that I met were friendly and intelligent, but I have to confess that, regarding the projects, nothing was taken ahead. Even in Haifa, where I designed an university, the same happened. I did the design in scale 1:500, delivered it, but the practice in charge of developing it never gave me any notice. I don't know, consequently, what happened to my design.

Still in Israel, they commissioned me to design a small village by the Negev Desert. It had to be compact. I began the study prescribing that the vehicles should stay out of the city, leaving it to the pedestrians who would be able to cross it walking from one side to the other. The 50-storey or more apartment buildings would be grouped off the city's periphery, linked to the indispensable parking areas and a big surrounding avenue. In the centre, we would have the administrative buildings, meeting and leisure areas, shops, theatres, cinemas. Close to the residential buildings, local shops and schools.

This Negev village was just an example, a fantasy, a hypothesis that, once realised in a more fertile site could extend lon-

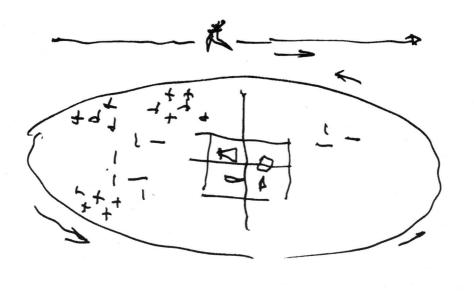

ind. / curio.

gitudinally, multipliable, like all cities should be, followed by parallel axis, destined to the industries, universities and agriculture.

I like the days I spent in Israel. My dear friend David Reznik, who worked with me in Rio and, nowadays, is a very competent architect in that country.

Wondered I have been around Eilat, nearly deserted, not yet suffocated by the real states' power, with only a few white lost spots in the landscape, and the desert's red sand mixing up the seawater.

~

For many years I travelled periodically abroad where I found support and friendship. André Malraux, as I said before, obtaining a special work permit from President De Gaulle, so that I could work in France like a French architect; Mondadori building up his headquarters in Milan and Boumedienne, passionate for my architecture, convoking me with enthusiasm: "You will be my consultant for architecture issues!" – he said.

I can't say those were happy days. On the contrary. During that unavoidable exile, one single word, any music that could possibly remind my country touched me with pity, making me remember my family and my friends far away, being persecuted by the dictatorship.

Of course I had my leisure moments, and I followed my friends in this laughing and crying that life is all about.

I remember the day when, desperate, I wrote down these verses, putting it on my office's wall.

I'm far from everything,
from everything I like,
from such a beautiful land,
that watched my birth.
One of these days I will explode,
I put my feet on down the road,
There, in Brazil,
Is where I want to live.
Each one on his place,
each one under his roof,
playing with his friends,
watching time passing by.
I want to watch the stars,
want to feel life,
There, in Brazil,
is where I want to live.
I'm so fucking angry,
this flu won't go away,
listening to so much rubbish,
I can't contain myself.
One of these days I explode,
and give it all up.
There, in Brazil,
Is where I want to live.
This place is not for me,
it's no use for me,
the decision is taken,
no one will stop me.
Fuck the job,
and this shit world,
there, in Brazil,
is where I want to live.

~

Time passed by. For years I haven't travelled abroad, and I occupy myself with the projects in Brazil. I would like to reduce my work, to choose only the most attractive ones, but many people depend on me, what obliges me to keep on the drawing board.

I came back to my office in Copacabana, and my working method is still the same. Defined one idea I write, as I said before, an explanatory text. And if I find valid arguments for it, I come back to the drawings. It's time to convoke the reinforced concrete technicians then. José Carlos Sussekind, Bruno Contarini or Fernando Rocha de Souza, and with them discussing the structural problems. After that I deliver the designs to those who will develop it, at the practice ran by my granddaughter Ana Elisa and her partner Jair Valera, or my nephew João Niemeyer's practice. They are competent, excellent architects – and they know my architecture. It is an easy step to me.

Obviously, from there on, we convoke other technicians – for lighting problems, Peter Gasper, acoustics, Nepomuceno, scenography, architect Robson. For furnishing jobs, my daughter Ana Maria.

These latest years I am the only architect in my office in Copacabana. Architecture has more and more become something personal to me. Other friends are part of the office, collaborating in parallel affairs – my grandson Carlos Oscar Niemeyer, Jayme Soares Brandão, Vera Lúcia Guimarães, Aurélio Bernardo de Araújo Osório and, eventually, Luís Otávio Ferreira Barreto Leite, who reviews my texts. My grandson Kadu Niemeyer is in charge of graphic design and photography. In another venue, in the Canoas house, my granddaughter Ana

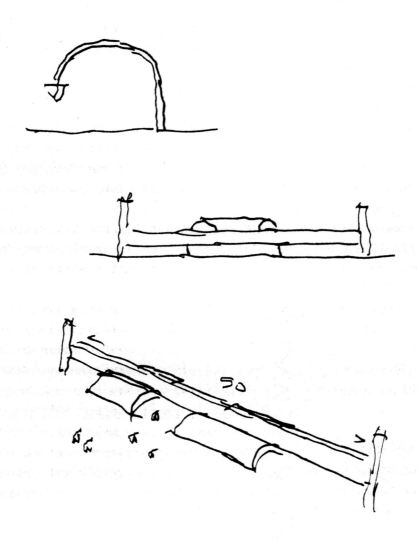

Lúcia runs the Oscar Niemeyer Foundation. And there is the indispensable support of Gilberto Antunes, the model maker.

In Brasilia, we count on the collaboration of Carlos Magalhães da Silveira, Fernando Andrade and Maria Amélia Mello Galvão. In São Paulo, Hélio Pasta, Hélio Penteado and Cecília Scharlach, who has recently organised a huge exhibition on my works, which will now travel the world.

Not rarely, my office is used for meetings of political character. It was in there that CEBRADE (Democratic Brazil Centre) was born — an institution that, under Renato Guimarães' direction, strongly actuated to fasten the end of the dictatorship in Brazil.

Life goes on and some new works came onto my hands. In São Paulo, the Latin American Memorial, already completed. In Brasilia, the last buildings of the "Monumental Axis". The Museum, the library, a big music hall, the planetarium and some cinemas.

In Rio, the Conventions Centre that Mayor Luís Paulo Conde intends to build up in Barra; the CIEPs[7] and the "Sambódromo"[8].

In Niterói, The Museum of Contemporary Art and the "Niemeyer Way" that Mayor Jorge Roberto Silveira dreams of carrying out. I'll detain myself on all these projects.

~

The Latin America Memorial design, commissioned by my friend governor Orestes Quercia, aimed to promote a better approach among the Latin American peoples. The Memorial comprehends the Acts Room, a library, an exhibition room, an

---

[7] Integrated Centre for Public Education.
[8] Sambadrome — Kind of open arena specially built for the yearly Samba Schools' Parade.

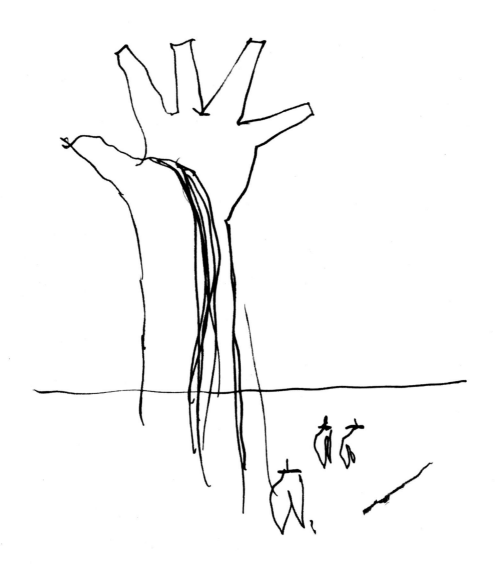

auditorium and the administrative building. The idea was to create a huge civic square, where people could meet. And the different buildings endowed with a more radical structure, like in the library, with its two supports outside the building, a 90 meters long beam, and the free space inside accepting any kind of solution.

Prevailing in the Memorial, the big white curved surfaces, repeated in favour of the unity. And at the square, the open hand that I designed, seven meters high, blood running down the fist, representing Latin America. It's a protest, an invitation to the indispensable fight against the successive menaces and interventions upon this continent.

The CIEP's in Rio de Janeiro are pre-fabricated public schools, and the most important thing about them is not the architecture but Darcy Ribeiro's idea of keeping children full time in there, guaranteeing meals, tranquillity, and peace to study, what they don't have at home. Regarding its architecture, we tried to make, even within the pre-fabricated, a remarkable structure, prominent in the neighbourhood, like important landmarks as really important this initiative is.

I remember the reactionary forces saying that the CIEPs were too much expensive, not realising how proud the children from the *favelas* enter them as if it constituted the beginning of a better life.

It was by that time that the schools made of reinforced mortar by João Filgueiras Lima, my dear friend Lelé, came out. So important in this genre of architecture that I could not forget.

On its turn, the design of the Sambódromo faced difficulties. The site was not ideal. The pre-existing Brahma [a beer company] building burdened a better solution. But this work brought us much satisfaction – it was made in three months

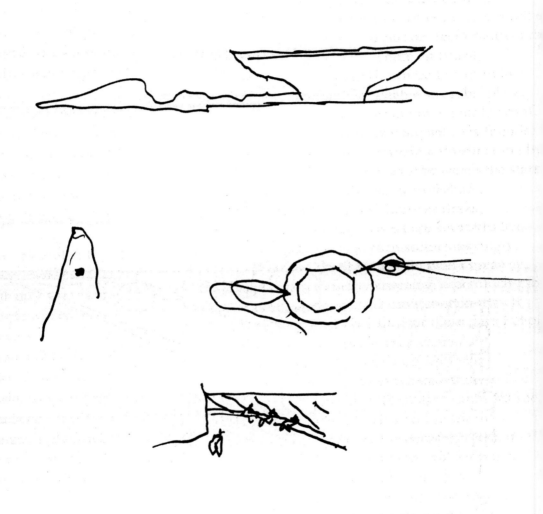

time only. Although destined to stalls, we achieved a more elegant solution to its structure, as shown in the photos.

In the case of the Contemporary Art Museum, in Niterói, the site is so beautiful that it was easy to design it. One central support, and architecture arising round about it, just like a flower. Then the ramp, inviting people to visit the museum, a walk around the architecture and the beautiful landscape, running under the building.

After the success achieved by this museum, Niterói city Mayor Jorge Roberto Silveira is thinking bigger. He is now possessed by the idea of building up what they call the Niemeyer Way, a row of buildings, by the sea, from the city centre as far as the Museum. The project will begin with a big square, by the water. One theatre, one convention centre, a memorial, a Catholic cathedral and a Protestant temple.

To make the construction viable, they scheduled five 20-storey apartment buildings. The venture attracted me: with buildings of such different destinations, it is an opportunity to create a modern development, where the reinforced concrete technique is presented by a good plastic freedom.

The theatre is also destined to open air public spectacles. For this reason we put the stage two meters above the ground level. By examining the longitudinal cut drawing on the page besides, first you will see the stage, then the audience and then the accesses. And following all these such different levels, the covering.

In architecture, when it is possible to explain a design with a small sketch, it's a proof that it's been well thought, as it always should be.

It is not the first time that I affirm – and it's worthy repeating it – my concern on, once finished the structure, architecture must already be present, simple and beautiful. Not

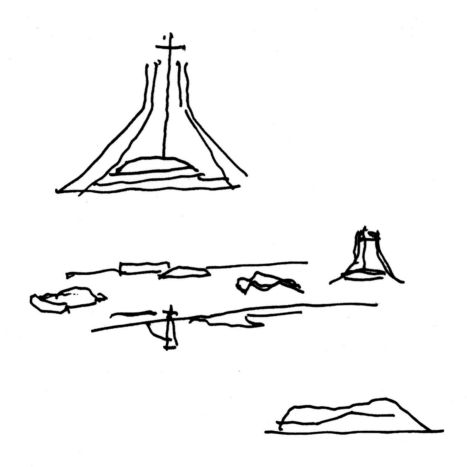

appealing to supports that will have to be hidden within the construction. It is the first step of creation, true and pure, as it imposes itself. In the case of this theatre, the design of its structure is so accurate that, having it done, it will be possible to use the theatre.

The conventions centre in Niterói is a big dome. On the ground level the exhibitions room, above it, an auditorium and completing the conjunct, a long two-storey building destined to a foundation.

The cathedral is so simple that it pleases me to explain. A 40X40 meters square, and four columns going up in a curve to a height of 30 meters. A volume that I imagined all in glass, what looked very nice in the sketches I did. But, unavoidably, problems with acoustics and the sun came up, making it difficult to keep, as I wished, the glass façades. But the solution suddenly occurred to me: A rod, a big concrete cupola – 30 meters in diameter, and the nave protected in a proper ambient of shadow and secrecy.

For a matter of unity, the Protestant temple, in spite of its circular shape, repeats the rod system adopted in the cathedral.

Completing the square, one bar, an area destined to pop music, and the little chapel that I designed on the water – linked to the square by a catwalk – kind of fantasy that sometimes gives a development like this, the desirable public interest.

By the beginning of this project I talked to the Mayor about the importance of convoking the artists.

I explained him it would be the opportunity of promoting, for the first time, the integration between arts and architecture in a more radical way. I told him that this matter always concerned me and that, since Pampulha, I always tried this collaboration, for me so much needed but never achieved, at least in the level that I wished, like in the Renascence heroic times.

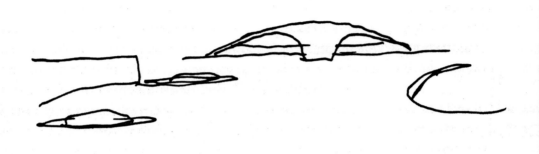

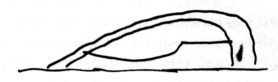

Understanding, he accepted my ideas, and it was arranged that, before starting the building works, he would call up the artists. And I started to review my design, with more accuracy, determining where I would put a sculpture, a mural painting, or a simple black and white drawing.

~

Another project that engages me at the moment is the big conventions centre that Mayor Luiz Paulo Conde intends to build up in Barra da Tijuca, west zone of Rio. It's composed by a 3.000 seats auditorium, two smaller 1.600 seats auditoriums and a supplementary building for general services.

The design of the main auditorium is ready and, what surprises me is to know that its architecture comes from a sketch that I did even before reaching the adopted solution. A landing white bird.

Actually what took me a lot of doing in this project was to find out a structural solution, so simple, so connected to the architecture that, once built up, it could show off all its greatness.

This concern that I always had on structures is understood by all the reinforced concrete technicians who I worked with so far. All first-rate ones. They have been so useful to me that I might quote some of them. Long ago, around 1936, Emílio Baumgart, then Fernando Souza and Joaquim Cardozo who, for many years worked with me; following, Bruno Catarini and lately, José Carlos Sussekind who, with his talent, sorts out all my fantasies.

~

Now, it is the Monumental Axis that engages me again. So far it has not been concluded, what afflicts us, anxious to see it finished under the same spirit of the architecture already built

85

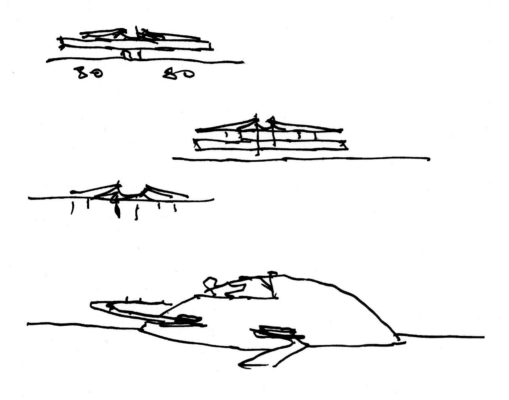

80   80

there. Due to the initiative of Governor Joaquim Roriz, there is now a new hope for us. I shall explain the latest designs I did and show how important they are, completing that axis with the indispensable "Cultural Sector".

The first design I did for the Brasilia Museum was of great structural audaciousness. A 180 meters long building, two central supports and 80 meters long overhangs held by rods. I was in Paris and went to Rome in order to show it to Pier Luigi Nervi. The great engineer smiled worried: "Niemeyer, you should have looked for me 10 years ago." But the idea captivated him, and he proposed metallic rods.

Time passed. Years. And when they decided to build up the design, for diverse reasons, the rods had to be in concrete. I consulted my friend José Carlos Sussekind, who did not hesitate, bringing me the calculations a few days later. Surprised to see him so at easy before such a technical problem I asked: "What if I create a garden on the block's rooftop" – I knew that it would complicate the solution. "What would happen?" And he answered promptly: "The rods make kind of an umbrella in which I can hang anything you want."

This episode tells us how up to date the engineering is in our country, ready to collaborate with our architecture.

Some years passed and, being the government interested in building up the museum, the design was brought up. After a long discussion, and despite the fact that many people like it, due to economy and mainly time reasons, I came up to another solution, which I explain next.

The New Brasilia Museum is then a big dome, 80 meters in diameter. The ground floor is destined to general services and houses a 1000 seats auditorium. On the first floor, the great salon, enriched by an irregular mezzanine and two glazed lifts. An external

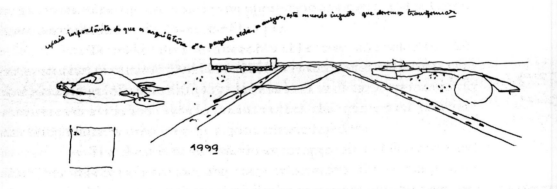

mais importante do que a arquitetura é a própria vida, os amigos, este mundo injusto que devemos transformar

1999

ramp with an overhang length of 15 meters, links the two floors spectacularly; and breaking the dome's geometry, on its top, a restaurant overlooking the landscape and the huge sky of the new capital.

And we included a school of art within the Museum's briefing, to promote the youth's initiation on the secrets of the artistic creation. This program made us create outside the Museum, by the square, a lowered protected area where children will be able to show off the talent that exists in them, spontaneously, free from the intervention of a limiting teaching.

We also designed a 100.000 volumes library, endowed with all the modern technical facilities such as computers, videos, auditoriums, reading rooms — open air ones inclusive — at last, all facilities a building of this kind must have.

The Music Hall houses a big salon, 80 meters in diameter, a central stage, outstanding stalls occupying different areas. The restaurant in the mezzanine that rounds about the big salon gives the audience, on the ground floor the necessary independence. The covering curves give the interior the wished amplitude and level differences.

The Planetarium constitutes such a technical problem, so limited it is by functional requirements that architecture has modestly influenced it. Plastically, the spherical shape was its natural solution, so beautiful that it was not worthy to avoid it.

The briefing still foresees 15 cinemas, bars, meeting rooms, toilettes, and we adapted ourselves to it, creating this large concrete plaque that completes and disciplines the complex.

All these buildings are part of the Monumental Axis. Museum and Library by one side, and the rest in the other. Realising them as soon as possible is our aim. How difficult it was to build up this city in such a short time, and mainly, how difficult it will be to conclude it in stages not breaking apart the architectural unity!

How nostalgic I am about the old times! The fraternal atmosphere that always involved us, the special ambience in which we lived, architects, engineers and workers. The discomfort and happiness that surrounded us , just like a fairer society was about to be born. What an Illusion! The politicians came, the money owners, and a wall of prejudices separated us again.

~

For many times I thought of doing sculptures. Huge ones free in the space. The sculptures I created so far always assumed a political character that, for me, justified them. One of them was against the violence in our country. Another against the murder of three workers by the militaries in Volta Redonda. This monument irritated them so much that by the night of its inauguration they destroyed it with bombs, such strong ones that the windows of the neighbour buildings had their glasses totally destroyed.

We came back to the site and recuperated the monument, leaving the scars as a reminder of the criminal assault. Another sculpture supported the Landlesses' Movement, it was also destroyed during the first confrontation with the policemen, but soon rebuilt, as part of their struggle for the land, which since long ago should belong to them.

On its turn, the one I designed for the Museé de la Resistence, in Paris, is still there, very well exposed. It reminds us that those who died during the Spanish civil war were, actually, in anticipation, the first victims of the war against the Nazism. The same happens to the hand I designed, seven meters high, for the Latin America Memorial, in São Paulo.

But it was only now, after so many years, that I decided to dedicate myself a bit more to the sculptures. I was chatting

90

with two friends in my office, artist Maurício Bentes and entre-preneur Rômulo Dantas, when, enthusiastic about the drawings that I had done, Rômulo proposed to fund them. And fifteen days later I was there, very in front of them — some are ab-stracts, others are completed by big sketches made of iron bars. Shortly after we were exhibiting them outside the Museum of Contemporary Art in Niterói.

The reviews were so generous that, since them, I con-sider myself qualified to this new artistry.

~

I read this book over and over and, defining my thoughts on architecture seems indispensable to me. I must say that I don't see my architecture as an ideal solution but, modestly, as my architecture. The one that I prefer, freer, full of curves, coura-geously penetrating this new world of forms that reinforced concrete brings us.

Saying that, for me, each architect must have his own architecture.

The idea of an ideal architecture, obedient, submitted to pre-established principles, would be the dissemination of medi-ocrity, monotony and repetition.

And to declare that the most important thing, in my point of view, is intuition. This intuition that goes on disclosesing the secrets of life, secrets of this so defenseless human being.

And it`s to preserve my intuition that I avoid reading about my architecture. It`s all alone, talking to myself, bending forward my drawing board, that for more than sixty years, I think and elaborate my architecture.

It`s not that I despise those who say so gentle words about my work. Instead, many are those who I admire, and for this very reason, I prefer not listening to them; although reading is a daily and permanent habit to me. How pleased I am to read a good romance, a good book about life, about the cosmo`s misteries; this universe so full of stars where, they say, one day we have come from.

Saint Francis' Chapel in Pampulha - Belo Horizonte

Tennis Club in Pampulha - Belo Horizonte

Casino in Pampulha - Belo Horizonte

Two views of the Alvorada Palace - Brasília

The Cathedral - Brasilia

Two views of the National Congress - Brasília

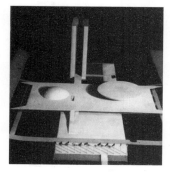

Congress' scale model

Three Powers Square - Brasilia

The Liberty Pantheon - Brasilia

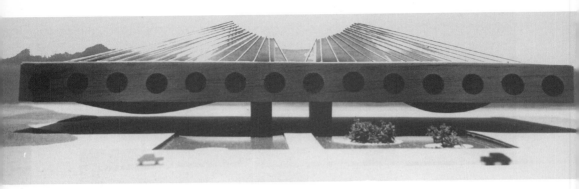

Music Hall - project - Rio de Janeiro

Residence at Canoas - Rio de Janeiro

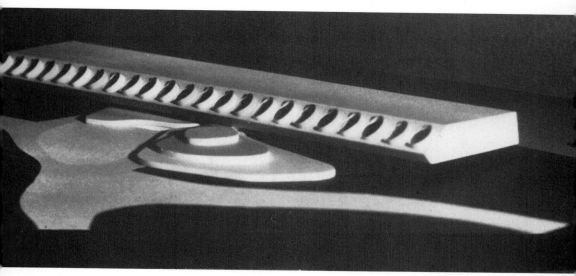

Oxford University - project - United Kingdom

Caracas Museum - project - Venezuela

Mondadori headquarters - Italy

French Communist Party`s headquarters - France

Job Centre in Bobigny - France

Espace Oscar Niemeyer - France

Espace Oscar Niemeyer - France

Alger Mosque - Algeria

University of Constantine - Algeria

University of Constantine   Alger Civic Centre - Algeria

Contemporary Art Museum - Niteroi

Oscar Niemeyer Way - project - Niteroi

Tecnet headquarters - project - Sao Paulo

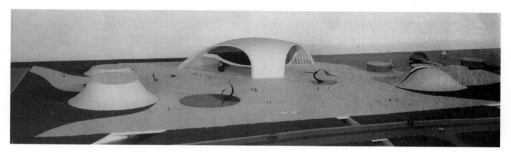

Cultural Centre in Barra da Tijuca - project - Rio de Janeiro

Visit our site
www.revan.com.br

Printed in Brazil

Editora Revan
Avenida Paulo de Frontin, 163
20260-010
Rio de Janeiro, RJ
Brasil

Telephone: +55 21 502 7495
Fax: +55 21 273 6873

E-mails:

editorial enquires:
editora@revan.com.br

sales:
vendarev@revan.com.br

press:
divulg@revan.com.br